## Dedication
To all those who ever struggled with learning a foreign language and to Wolfgang Karfunkel

## Also by Yatir Nitzany

Conversational Spanish Quick and Easy

Conversational French Quick and Easy

Conversational Italian Quick and Easy

Conversational Portuguese Quick and Easy

Conversational German Quick and Easy

Conversational Dutch Quick and Easy

Conversational Norwegian Quick and Easy

Conversational Danish Quick and Easy

Conversational Russian Quick and Easy

Conversational Ukrainian Quick and Easy

Conversational Bulgarian Quick and Easy

Conversational Polish Quick and Easy

Conversational Hebrew Quick and Easy

Conversational Yiddish Quick and Easy

Conversational Armenian Quick and Easy

Conversational Arabic Quick and Easy

# Conversational French Quick and Easy
## The Most Innovative Technique to Learn the French Language

# Part III

### YATIR NITZANY

Translated by:
Semadar Mercedes Friedman

Interior Design:
Menachem Otto

Copyright © 2019
Yatir Nitzany
All rights reserved.
ISBN 13: 978-1951244491
Printed in the United States of America

# Foreword

## About Myself

For many years I struggled to learn Spanish, and I still knew no more than about twenty words. Consequently, I was extremely frustrated. One day I stumbled upon this method as I was playing around with word combinations. Suddenly, I came to the realization that every language has a certain core group of words that are most commonly used and, simply by learning them, one could gain the ability to engage in quick and easy conversational Spanish.

I discovered which words those were, and I narrowed them down to three hundred and fifty that, once memorized, one could connect and create one's own sentences. The variations were and are *infinite*! By using this incredibly simple technique, I could converse at a proficient level and speak Spanish. Within a week, I astonished my Spanish-speaking friends with my newfound ability. The next semester I registered at my university for a Spanish language course, and I applied the same principles I had learned in that class (grammar, additional vocabulary, future and past tense, etc.) to those three hundred and fifty words I already had memorized, and immediately I felt as if I had grown wings and learned how to fly.

At the end of the semester, we took a class trip to San José, Costa Rica. I was like a fish in water, while the rest of my classmates were floundering and still struggling to converse. Throughout the following months, I again applied the same principle to other languages—French, Portuguese, Italian, and Arabic, all of which I now speak proficiently, thanks to this very simple technique.

This method is by far the fastest way to master quick and easy conversational language skills. There is no other technique that compares to my concept. It is effective, it worked for me, and it will work for you. Be consistent with my program, and you too will succeed the way I and many, many others have.

# Table of Contents

Introduction to the Program .................................................................9

Introduction to the French Language ..................................................11

Memorization Made Easy.....................................................................12

The Program
- Office............................................................................... 15
- School.............................................................................. 19
- Profession ....................................................................... 21
- Business .......................................................................... 25
- Sports .............................................................................. 29
- Outdoor Activities ......................................................... 33
- Electric............................................................................. 35
- Tools ................................................................................ 37
- Auto ................................................................................. 41
- Nature ............................................................................. 43
- Animals ........................................................................... 45
- Religion ........................................................................... 49
- Wedding and Relationship ........................................... 53
- Politics ............................................................................. 49
- Military ........................................................................... 53

Basic Grammatical Requirements of the French Language....................57

Conclusion............................................................................................63

Note from the Author ..........................................................................64

# Introduction to the Program

You have now reached Part 3 of Conversational French Quick and Easy. In Part 1 you learned the 350 words that could be used in an infinite number of combinations. In Part 2 you moved on to putting these words into sentences. You learned how to ask for help when your house was hit by a hurricane and how to find the emergency services. For example, if you need to go to a hospital, you have now been provided with sentences and the vocabulary for talking to doctors and nurses and dealing with surgery and health issues. When you get to the hospital, you can tell the health services, "The hurricane caused a lot of destruction and damage in its path," and "We used the hurricane shelter for refuge."

In this third book in the series, you will find the culmination of this foreign language course that is based on a system using key phrases used in day-to-day life. You can now move on to further topics such as things you would say in an office. This theme is ideal if you've just moved to French for a new job. You may be about to sit at your desk to do an important task assigned to you by your boss but you have forgotten the details you were given. Turn to your colleagues and say, "I have to write an important email but I forgot my password." Then, if the reply is "Our secretary isn't here today. Only the receptionist is here but she is in the bathroom," you'll know what is being said and you can wait for help. By the end of the first few weeks, you'll have at your disposal terminology that can help reflect your experiences. "I want to retire already," you may find yourself saying at coffee break on a Monday morning after having had to go to your bank manager and say, "I need a small loan in order to pay my mortgage this month."

I came up with the idea of this unique system of learning foreign languages as I was struggling with my own attempt to learn French. When playing around with word combinations I discovered 350 words that when used together could make up an infinite number of sentences. From this beginning, I was able to start speaking in a new language. I then practiced and found that I could use the same technique with other languages, such as French, Portuguese, Italian and Arabic. It was a revelation.

This method is by far the easiest and quickest way to master other languages and begin practicing conversational language skills.

The range of topics and the core vocabulary are the main components of this flawless learning method. In Part 3 you have a chance to learn how to relate to people in many more ways. Sports, for example, are very important for keeping healthy and in good spirits. The social component of these types of activities should not be underestimated at all. You will, therefore, have much help when you meet some new people, perhaps in a bar, and want to say to them, "I like to watch basketball games," and "Today are the finals of the Olympic Games. Let's see who wins the World Cup."

For sports, the office, and for school, some parts of conversation are essential. What happens when you need to get to work but don't have any clean clothes to wear because of malfunctions with the machinery. What you need is to be able to pick up the phone and ask a professional or a friend, "My washing machine and dryer are broken so maybe I can wash my laundry at the public laundromat." When you finally head out after work for some drinks and meet a nice new man, you can say, "You can leave me a voicemail or send me a text message."

Hopefully, these examples help show you how reading all three parts of this series in combination will prepare you for all you need in order to boost your conversational learning skills and engage with others in your newly learned language. The first two books have been an important start. This third book adds additional vocabulary and will provide the comprehensive knowledge required.

# The French Language

The French language originated in France. It is a Romance language as are Spanish, Portuguese, Italian, and Romanian since they all descend from what originally was the spoken Latin language. In the sixteenth century, King Francis I declared French as his nation's official language. Little did he know it was soon to become the fifteenth most-common language in the world and the official language of almost thirty countries.

The French language was once used in diplomatic circles and was also a symbol of prestige, meaning only the nobility and higher classes of educated people spoke it. Russia's Catherine the Great and all her court communicated in French, as well as Prussia's Frederick II. Today, because of France's colonial expansion between the seventeenth and twentieth centuries, there are now twenty-nine countries where French is the official language. Despite its many dialects French is still spoken in all its former colonies. However, the language has declined in popularity since its peak in the sixteen and seventeenth centuries. But French is again rising in popularity. It has sixteen million students and 220 million native speakers.

## Memorization Made Easy

There is no doubt the three hundred and fifty words in my program are the required essentials in order to engage in quick and easy basic conversation in any foreign language. However, some people may experience difficulty in the memorization. For this reason, I created Memorization Made Easy. This memorization technique will make this program so simple and fun that it's unbelievable! I have spread the words over the following twenty pages. Each page contains a vocabulary table of ten to fifteen words. Below every vocabulary box, sentences are composed from the words on the page that you have just studied. This aids greatly in memorization. Once you succeed in memorizing the first page, then proceed to the second page. Upon completion of the second page, go back to the first and review. Then proceed to the third page. After memorizing the third, go back to the first and second and repeat. And so on. As you continue, begin to combine words and create your own sentences in your head. Every time you proceed to the following page, you will notice words from the previous pages will be present in those simple sentences as well, because repetition is one of the most crucial aspects in learning any foreign language. Upon completion of your twenty pages, *congratulations,* you have absorbed the required words and gained a basic, quick-and-easy proficiency and you should now be able to create your own sentences and say anything you wish in the French language. This is a crash course in conversational French, and it works!

# The Program "*Conversational French Quick and Easy*" Let's Begin

# OFFICE - BUREAU

**Boss - (male)** Patron/ **(female)** patronne
**Employee -** Employé / **(female)** employée
**Staff -** Personnel
**Meeting -** Réunion
**Conference room -** Salle de conférence
**Secretary -** Secrétaire / **Receptionist -** Réceptionniste
**Schedule -** Programme
**Calendar -** Calendrier
**Supplies -** Provisions
**Pen -** Stylo / **Ink -** Encre
**Pencil -** Crayon / **Eraser -** La gomme
**Desk -** Bureau / **Cubicle -** Cabine / **Chair -** Chaise
**Office furniture -** Meubles de bureau
**Business card -** Carte de visite
**Lunch break -** Heure du déjeuner
**Days off -** Jours de congés
**Briefcase -** Mallette
**Bathroom -** Salle de bains

**My boss asked me to hand in the paperwork.**
Mon patron m'a demandé de remettre les documents.
**Our secretary isn't here today. The receptionist is here but she is in the bathroom.**
Notre secrétaire n'est pas ici aujourd'hui. La réceptionniste est là mais elle est dans la salle de bain.
**The employee meeting can take place in the conference room.**
La réunion des employés peut avoir lieu dans la salle de conférence.
**My business cards are inside my briefcase.**
Mes cartes de visite sont dans ma mallette.
**The office staff must check their work schedule daily.**
Le personnel du bureau doit vérifier quotidiennement son horaire de travail.
**I am going to buy office furniture.**
Je vais acheter des muebles de bureau.
**There isn't any ink in this pen.**
Il n'y a pas d'encre dans ce stylo.
**This pencil is missing an eraser.**
Ce crayon manque une gomme.
**Our days off are written on the calendar.**
Nos jours de congé sont inscrits sur le calendrier.
**I need to buy extra office supplies.**
J'ai besoin d'acheter matériel supplémentaires de bureau.
**I am busy until lunch.**
Je suis occupé jusqu'à ma déjeuner.

**Laptop -** Ordinateur portable
**Computer -** Ordinateur
**Keyboard -** Clavier
**Mouse -** Souris
**Email -** Email
**Password -** Mot de passe
**Attachment -** Attachement
**Printer -** Imprimante
**Colored printer -** Imprimante en couleur
**To download -** Télécharger
**To upload -** Télécharger
**Internet -** l'Internet
**Account -** Compte
**A copy -** Une copie / **To copy -** Copier
**Paste -** Coller
**Cut and paste -** Couper et coller
**Fax -** Fax
**Scanner -** Scanner / **To scan -** Scanner
**Telephone -** Téléphone
**A charger -** Une chargeur / **To charge -** Charger

**I have to write an important email but I forgot my password for my account.**
Je dois écrire un e-mail important mais j'ai oublié mon mot de passe pour mon compte.
**I need to purchase a computer, a keyboard, a printer, and a desk.**
Je dois acheter un ordinateur, un clavier, une imprimante et un bureau.
**Where is the mouse for my laptop?**
Où est la souris de mon ordinateur portable?
**The internet is slow today therefore it's difficult to upload or download.**
L'nternet est lent aujourd'hui, et cest donc difficile de le télécharger.
**Do you have a colored printer?**
Avez-vous une imprimante de couleur?
**I needed to fax the contract but instead, I decided to send it as an attachment in the email.**
J'avais besoin de faxer le contrat mais au lieu de ca, j'ai décidé de l'envoyer en pièce jointe dans l'e-mail.
**One of these days, the fax machine will be completely obsolete.**
Un de ces jours, le télécopieur sera complètement obsolète.
**Where is my phone charger?**
Où est mon chargeur de téléphone?
**The scanner is broken.**
Le scanner est cassé.
**The telephone is behind the chair.**
Le téléphone est derrière la chaise.

# Office

**Shredder -** Destructeur / déchiqueteur
**Copy machine -** Photocopieuse
**Filing cabinet -** Armoire de classement
**Paper -** Papier **/ Page -** Page
**Paperwork -** Formalités administratives
**Portfolio -** Portefeuille
**Files -** Des dossiers
**Document -** Document
**Contract -** Contrat
**Records -** Records
**Archives -** Les archives
**Deadline -** Date limite
**Binder -** Classeur
**Paper clip -** Trombone
**Stapler -** Agrafeuse **/ Staples -** Agrafes
**Stamp -** Timbre
**Mail -** Courrier
**Letter -** Lettre
**Envelope -** Enveloppe
**Data -** Les données
**Analysis -** Une analyse
**Highlighter -** Surligneur **/ Marker -** Marqueur **/ To highlight -** Souligner
**Ruler -** Règle

**The supervisor at our company is responsible for data analysis.**
Le superviseur de notre entreprise est responsable de l'analyse des données.
**The copy machine is next to the telephone.**
Le copieur est à côté du téléphone.
**The ruler is next to the shredder.**
La règle est à côté du déchiqueteur.
**I can't find my stapler, paper clips, nor my highlighter in my cubicle.**
Je ne trouve pas mon agrafeuse, mes trombones ni mon surligneur dans ma cabine.
**The filing cabinet is full of documents.**
Le classeur est plein des documents.
**The garbage can is full of papers.**
La poubelle est pleine des papiers.
**Give me the file because today is the deadline.**
Donnez-moi le dossier car c'est aujourd'hui la date limite.
**Where do I put the binder?**
Où dois-je mettre le classeur?
**I need a stamp and an envelope.**
J'ai besoin d'un timbre et d'une enveloppe.
**There is a letter in the mail.**
Il y a une lettre dans le courrier.

# SCHOOL - ÉCOLE

**Student -** Étudiant / **(f)** étudiante
**Teacher -** Enseignant / **(f)** professeure
**Substitute teacher -** Enseignant suppléant
**A class -** Une classe
**A classroom -** Une salle de classe
**Education -** Éducation
**Private school -** Ecole privée
**Public school -** École publique
**Elementary school -** École primaire
**Middle school -** Collège
**High school -** Lycée
**University -** Université / **College -** College
**Grade** (level) **-** Grade / **Grade** (grade on a test) **-** Note
**Pass -** Passe / **Fail -** Échouer
**Absent -** Absent / **Present -** Présent

**The classroom is empty.**
La salle de classe est vide.
**I want to bring my laptop to class today.**
Je veux amener mon ordinateur portable en classe aujourd'hui.
**Our math teacher is absent and therefore a substitute teacher replaced him.**
Notre professeur de mathématiques est absent et donc un professeur suppléant l'a remplacé.
**All the students are present.**
Tous les étudiants sont présents.
**Make sure to pass your classes because you can't fail this semester.**
Assurez-vous de réussir vos cours, car vous ne pouvez pas échouer ce semestre.
**The education level at a private school is much more intense.**
Le niveau d'éducation dans une école privée est beaucoup plus intense.
**I went to a public elementary and middle school.**
Je suis allé dans une école primaire et secondaire publique.
**I have good memories of high school.**
J'ai des bons souvenirs du lycée.
**You must get good grades on your report card.**
Vous devez obtenir des bonnes notes sur votre bulletin.
**My son is 15 years old and he is in the ninth grade.**
Mon fils a 15 ans et il est en sa neuvième année.
**College textbooks are expensive.**
Les manuels universitaires sont chers.
**I want to study at an out-of-state university.**
Je veux étudier dans une université étrangère.

**Subject -** Sujet
**Science -** Science / **Chemistry -** Chimie / **Physics -** Physique
**Geography -** Géographie
**History -** Histoire
**Math -** Math
**Addition -** Addition
**Subtraction -** Soustraction
**Division -** Division
**Multiplication -** Multiplication
**Language -** Langue / **English -** Anglais / **Foreign language -** Langue étrangère
**Physical education -** Éducation physique
**Chalk -** Craie/ **Board -** Tableau
**Report card -** Fiche de rendement
**Alphabet -** Alphabet / **Letters -** Lettres/ **Words -** Mots
**To review -** À revoir
**Dictionary -** Dictionnaire
**Detention -** Détention
**The principle -** Le directeur

**At school, geography is my favorite subject, English is easy, math is hard, and history is boring.**
À l'école, la géographie est ma matière préférée, l'anglais est facile, les mathématiques sont difficiles et l'histoire est ennuyeuse.
**After English class, there is physical education.**
Après les cours d'anglais, il y a l'éducation physique.
**Today's math lesson is on addition and subtraction. Next month it will be division and multiplication.**
La leçon de mathématiques d'aujourd'hui porte sur l'addition et la soustraction. Le mois prochain, ce sera la division et la multiplication.
**This year for foreign language credits, I want to choose Spanish and French.**
Cette année pour les crédits en langues étrangères, je veux choisir l'espagnol et le français.
**I want to buy a dictionary, thesaurus, and a journal for school.**
Je veux acheter un dictionnaire, un thésaurus et un journal pour l'école.
**The teacher needs to write the homework on the board with chalk.**
L'enseignant doit écrire les devoirs au tableau avec la craie.
**Today the students have to review the letters of the alphabet**
Aujourd'hui, les étudiants doivent revoir les lettres de l'alphabet
**The teacher wants to teach roman numerals.**
L'professeur veut enseigner les chiffres romains.
**If you can't behave then you must go to the principal's office, and maybe stay after school for detention.**
Si vous ne pouvez pas vous comporter, vous devez vous rendre au bureau du directeur et peut-être rester après l'école pour la détention.

## School

**Test** - Examen / **Quiz** - Quiz
**Lesson** - Leçon / **Notes** - Notes
**Homework** - Devoirs / **Assignment** - Affectation / **Project** - Projet
**Pencil** - Crayon / **Pen** - Stylo / **Ink** - Encre / **Eraser** - La gomme
**Backpack** - Sac à dos
**Book** - Livre / **Folders** - Dossiers/ **Notebook** - Notebook / **Papers** - Papiers
**Calculator** - Calculatrice
**Glue** - Colle / **Adhesive tape** - Ruban adhésif / **Scissors** - Ciseaux
**Lunchbox** - Boîte à déjeuner / **Lunch** - Déjeuner/ **Cafeteria** - Cafétéria
**Kindergarten** - Jardin d'enfants / **Pre-school** - Préscolaire
**Day care** - Garderies, la creche
**Triangle** - Triangle / **Square** - Carré/ **Circle** - Circle
**Crayons** - Crayons de couleur

**Today, we don't have a test but we have a surprise quiz.**
Aujourd'hui, nous n'avons pas d'examen mais nous avons un quiz surprise.
**Are a pen, a pencil, and an eraser included with the school supplies?**
Est-ce que un stylo, un crayon et une gomme sont-ils inclus avec les fournitures scolaires?
**I think my notepad and calculator are in my backpack.**
Je pense que mon bloc-notes et ma calculatrice sont dans mon sac à dos.
**All my papers are in my folder.**
Tous mes papiers sont dans mon dossier.
**I need glue and scissors for my project.**
J'ai besoin de colle et de ciseaux pour mon projet.
**I need tape and a stapler to fix my book.**
J'ai besoin de ruban adhésif et d'une agrafeuse pour réparer mon livre.
**You have to concentrate in order to take notes.**
Il faut se concentrer pour prendre des notes.
**The school librarian wants to invite the art and music teacher to the library next week.**
Le bibliothécaire de l'école veux inviter le professeur d'art et de musique à la bibliothèque la semaine prochaine.
**For lunch, your children can purchase food at the cafeteria or they can bring food from home.**
Pour le déjeuner, vos enfants peuvent acheter de la nourriture à la cafétéria ou apporter de la nourriture de la maison.
**I forgot my lunchbox and crayons at home.**
J'ai oublié ma boîte de déjuner et mes crayons à la maison.
**To draw shapes such as a triangle, square, circle, and rectangle is easy.**
Il est facile de dessiner des formes telles qu'un triangle, un carré, un cercle et un rectangle.
**During the week, my youngest child is at daycare, my middle one is in pre-school, and the oldest is in kindergarten.**
Pendant la semaine, mon plus jeune enfant est à la garderie, mon deuxième est à la préscolaire et le plus âgé est au jardin d'enfants.

# PROFESSION - PROFESSION

**Doctor** - Docteur, médecin / **Nurse** - Infirmier, **(f)** infirmière
**Psychologist** - Psychologue / **Psychiatrist** - Psychiatre
**Veterinarian** - Vétérinaire
**Lawyer** - Avocat, avocate / **Judge** - Juge
**Pilot** - Pilote / **Flight attendant** - Agent de bord
**Reporter** - Journaliste / **Journalist** - Journaliste
**Electrician** - Électricien / **Mechanic** - Mécanicien
**Investigator** - Enquêteur / **Detective** - Détective
**Translator** - Traducteur / **(f)** traductrice
**Producer** - Producteur / **Director** - Réalisateur

**What's your profession?**
Quelle est votre profession?
**I am going to medical school to study medicine because I want to be a doctor.**
Je vais à l'école de médecine pour étudier la médecine parce que je veux être médecin.
**There is a difference between a psychologist and a psychiatrist.**
Il y a une différence entre un psychologue et un psychiatre.
**Most children want to be an astronaut, a veterinarian, or an athlete.**
La plupart des enfants veulent être des astronautes, ou bien vétérinaires ou athlètes.
**The judge spoke to the lawyer at the court house.**
Le juge a parlé avec l'avocat du palais de justice.
**The police investigator needs to investigate this case.**
L'enquêteur de police doit enquêter sur cette affaire.
**Being a detective could be a fun job.**
Être détective pourrait être un travail amusant.
**The flight attendant and the pilot are on the plane.**
L'hôtesse de l'air et le pilote sont dans l'avion.
**I am a certified electrician.**
Je suis électricien certifié.
**The mechanic overcharged me.**
Le mécanicien m'a surfacturé.
**I want to be a journalist.**
Je veux être un journaliste.
**The best translators work at my company.**
Les meilleurs traducteurs travaillent dans ma entreprise.
**Are you a photographer?**
Êtes-vous un photographe?
**The author wants to write a book.**
L'auteur veut écrire un livre.
**I want to find the directors of the company.**
Je veux trouver les dirigeants de l'entreprise.

**Artist** (performer) **-** Artiste
**Artist** (draws paints picture) **-** Artiste
**Author -** Auteur **/ (f)** auteure
**Painter -** Peintre
**Dancer -** Danseur **/ (f)** danseuse
**Writer -** Écrivain **/ (f)** écrivaine
**Photographer -** Photographe
**A cook -** Un cuisinier / un chef
**Waiter -** Serveur
**Bartender -** Barman
**Barber shop -** Salon de coiffure **/ Barber -** Coiffeur **/ (f)** coiffeuse
**Stylist -** Stylist
**Housekeeper -** La gouvernante **/ Maid -** Femme de ménage **/ Caretaker -** Le concierge
**Farmer -** Fermier **/ Agriculturer -** Agriculteur
**Gardner -** Jardinier
**Mailman -** Facteur
**A guard -** Un garde
**A cashier -** Un caissier

**The artist drew a sketch.**
L'artiste a dessiné un croquis.
**The artist produced new artwork for her catalog.**
L'artiste a produit de nouvelles illustrations pour son catalogue.
**I want to apply as a cook at the restaurant instead of as a waiter.**
Je veux postuler comme cuisinier au restaurant plutôt que serveur.
**The gardener can only come on weekdays.**
Le jardinier ne peut venir qu'en pendant las jours de travail.
**I have to go to the barbershop now.**
Je dois y aller au salon de coiffure maintenant.
**Being a bartender isn't an easy job.**
Être un barman n'est pas une tâche facile.
**Why do we need another maid?**
Pourquoi avons-nous besoin d'une autre femme de chambre?
**I need to file a complaint against the mailman.**
Je dois porter plainte contre le facteur.
**I am a part-time painter.**
Je suis un peintre à temps partiel.
**She was a dancer at the theater play.**
Elle était une danseuse à la pièce de theatre.
**You need to contact the insurance company if you want to find another caretaker.**
Vous devez contacter la compagnie d'assurance si vous voulez trouver un autre gardien.
**The farmer can sell us ripened tomatoes today.**
L'agriculteur peut nous vendre des tomates mûres aujourd'hui.

# BUSINESS - ENTREPRISE

**A business -** Entreprise / **Company -** Entreprise / **Factory -** Fabrique, usine
**A professional -** Un professionnel / **Position -** Position
**Work, job -** Un travail, un boulo
**Employee -** Employé / **(f)** employée
**Manager -** Directeur, **(f)** directrice / **Management -** La gestion / **Owner -** Propriétaire
**Secretary -** Secrétaire
**An interview -** Un entretien / **Résumé -** Résumé, curriculum vitae
**Presentation -** Presentation
**Specialist -** Spécialiste
**To hire -** Engager / **To fire -** Renvoyer, de licencier
**Pay check -** Chèque de paie / **Income -** Le revenu / **Salary -** Un salaire
**Insurance -** Assurance / **Benefits -** Avantages
**Trimester -** Trimestre / **Budget -** Budget
**Net -** Net / **Gross -** Brut
**To retire -** Prendre sa retraite, etre en pension / **Pension -** Pension

**I need a job.**
J'ai besoin d'un boulo.
**She is the secretary of the company.**
Elle est la secrétaire de l'entreprise.
**The manager needs to hire another employee.**
Le gestionnaire doit engager un autre employé.
**I am lucky because I have an interview for a cashier position today.**
J'ai de la chance car j'ai aujourd'hui un entretien pour un poste de caissier.
**How much is the salary and does it include benefits?**
Combien est le salaire et ça comprend-il les avantages sociaux?
**Management has your resumé and they need to show it to the owner of the company.**
La direction a votre curriculum vitae et ils doivent le montrer au propriétaire de l'entreprise.
**I am at work at the factory now.**
Je suis au travaille maintenant à l'usine.
**In business, you should be professional.**
En affaires, vous devez être professionnel.
**Is the presentation ready?**
Est-ce que la présentation est prête?
**The first trimester is part of the annual budget.**
Le premier trimestre fait partie du budget annuel.
**I have to see the net and gross profits of the business.**
Je dois voir les bénéfices nets et bruts de l'entreprise.
**I want to retire already.**
Je veux déjà prendre ma retraite.

**Client -** Client **/ (f)** cliente
**Broker -** Courtier **/ Salesperson -** Vendeur **/ (f)** vendeuse
**Realtor -** Agent immobilier **/ Real Estate -** Immobilier
**A purchase** - Un achat **/ A lease -** Un bail **/ To lease -** À louer
**To invest -** Investir **/ Investment -** Investissement
**Economy -** Économie
**Mortgage -** Hypothèque **/ Interest rate -** Taux d'intérêt **/ A loan -** Un prêt
**Commission -** Commission **/ Percent -** Pour cent **/ Value -** Valeur
**A sale -** Une vente
**Profit -** Profit
**Landlord -** Propriétaire **/ Tenant -** Locataire
**The demand -** La demande **/ The supply -** L'offre
**A contract -** Un contrat**/ Terms -** Termes **/ Signature -** Signature **/ Initials -** Initiales
**Stock -** Bourse **/ Stock broker -** Courtier en bourse
**Advertisement -** Publicité **/ Ads -** Les publicités

**I can earn a huge profit from the stock market.**
Je peux faire un énorme profit au marché boursier.
**The demand in the real estate market depends on the economy.**
La demande sur le marché immobilier dépend de l'économie.
**If you want to sell your home, I can recommend a very good realtor.**
Si vous voulez vendre votre maison, je peux vous recommander un très bon agent immobilier.
**The investor wants to invest in this shopping center because he says it has good potential.**
L'investisseur veut investir dans ce centre commercial car il dit qu'il a un bon potentiel.
**The value of the property increased by twenty percent.**
La valeur de la propriété a augmenté de vingt pour cent.
**How much is the commission on the sale?**
Combien coûte la commission de la vente?
**The client wants to lease instead of purchasing the property.**
Le client veut louer au lieu d'acheter la propriété.
**What are the terms of the purchase?**
Quelles sont les conditions d'achat?
**I can negotiate a better interest rate.**
Je peux négocier des meilleurs taux d'intérêt.
**I need a small loan in order to pay my mortgage this month.**
J'ai besoin d'un petit prêt pour payer mon hypothèque ce mois-ci.
**I need a signature and an initial on the contract.**
J'ai besoin d'une signature et des initiales sur le contrat.
**My position in the company is marketing and I am responsible for advertising and ads.**
Mon poste dans l'entreprise est le marketing et je suis responsable de la publicité et des anonces.

# Business

**Money** - Argent / **Currency** - Devise
**Cash** - En espèces / **Coins** - Pièces de monnaie
**Change** (change for a bill) - Monnaie
**Credit** - Crédit
**Tax** - Impôt
**Price** - Prix
**Invoice** - Facture d'achat
**Inventory** - Inventaire
**Merchandise** - Marchandise
**A refund** - Un remboursement
**A product** - Un produit
**Produced** - Produit
**Retail** - Détail
**Wholesale** - En gros
**Imports** - Importations / **Exports** - Exportations
**To ship** - Envoyer
**Shipment** - Expédition

**Don't forget to bring cash with you.**
N'oubliez pas d'apporter de l'argent avec vous.
**Do you have change for a $100 bill?**
Avez-vous de la monnaie pour un billet de 100?
**I don't have a credit card.**
Je n'ai pas de carte de crédit.
**The salesperson told me there is no refund.**
Le vendeur m'a dit qu'il n'y avait pas de remboursement.
**This product is produced in Italy.**
Ce produit est fabriqué en Italie.
**I work in the export/import business.**
Je travaille dans l'exportation / importation.
**Let me check my inventory.**
Permettez-moi de vérifier mon inventaire.
**This product is covered by insurance.**
Ce produit est couvert par une assurance.
**This invoice contains a mistake.**
Cette facture contient une erreur.
**What is the wholesale and retail value of this shipment?**
Quelle est la valeur en gros et au détail de cette expédition?
**You don't have enough money to purchase the merchandise.**
Vous n'avez pas assez d'argent pour acheter la marchandise.
**How much does the shipping cost and is it in US currency?**
Combien coûte l'expédition et est-elle en devise américaine?
**There is a tax exemption on this income.**
Il existe une exonération fiscale sur ces revenus.

## SPORTS - DES SPORTS

**Basketball -** Basketball / **Soccer -** Football
**Game -** Jeu / **Stadium -** Stade / **Ball -** Balle
**Player -** Joueur / **(f)** joueuse
**To jump -** Sauter / **To throw -** Lancer / **To kick -** Coup de pied / **To catch -** Attraper
**Coach -** Entraîneur, **(f)** entraîneuse / **Referee -** Arbitre
**Competition -** Compétition
**Team -** Équipe / **Teammate -** Coéquipier
**National team -** Équipe nationale
**Opponent -** Adversaire
**Half time -** Mi-temps / **Finals -** Finales
**Score -** But / **Scores -** Les scores
**Goal -** Objectif / **The goal -** Le but
**To lose -** Perdre / **A Defeat -** Une défaite / **To win -** Gagner / **A victory -** Une victoire
**The looser -** Détendus / **The winner -** Le gagnant
**Fans -** Amateurs
**Field -** Champ
**Helmet -** Casque / **Whistle -** Un sifflet
**Penalty -** Peine
**Basket -** Panier

**I like to watch basketball games.**
J'aime regarder des matchs de basket.
**Soccer is my favorite sport.**
Le football est mon sport préféré.
**I have tickets to a football game at the stadium.**
J'ai des billets pour un match de football au stade.
**To play basketball, you need to be good at shooting and jumping.**
Pour jouer au basket-ball, vous devez être bon au tir et au saut.
**The national team has a lot of fans.**
L'équipe nationale a beaucoup des amateurs.
**My teammate can't find his baseball helmet.**
Mon coéquipier ne trouve pas son casque de baseball.
**The coach and the team were on the field during half-time.**
L'entraîneur et l'équipe étaient sur le terrain au mi-temps.
**The coach needs to bring his team today to meet the new referee.**
L'entraîneur doit amener son équipe aujourd'hui pour rencontrer le nouvel arbitre.
**Our opponents went home after their defeat.**
Nos adversaires sont rentrés chez eux après leur défaite.
**The player received a penalty for kicking the ball in the wrong goal.**
Le joueur a reçu une pénalité pour avoir botté le ballon dans le mauvais but.
**Not every person likes sports.**
Pas tout le monde aime le sport.

**Athlete -** Athlète
**Olympics -** Jeux olympiques / **World cup -** Coupe du monde
**Bicycle -** Vélo / **Cyclist -** Cycliste / **Swimming -** Nager
**Wrestling -** Lutte / **Boxing -** Boxe / **Martial arts -** Arts martiaux
**Championship -** Championnat / **Award -** Prix / **Tournament -** Tournoi
**Horse racing -** Courses hippiques / **Racing -** Courses
**Exercise -** Exercice / **Fitness -** Aptitude, remise en forme / **Gym -** Gym
**Captain -** Capitain / **Judge -** Juge
**A match -** Un match / **Rules -** Règles / **Track -** Piste
**Trainer -** Entraîneur, **(f)** entraîneuse
**Pool** (billiards) **-** Billard / **Pool** (swimming pool) **-** La piscine

**Today are the finals for the Olympic Games.**
Aujourd'hui sont les finales des Jeux Olympiques.
**Let's see who wins the World Cup.**
Voyons qui gagne la Coupe du monde.
**I want to compete in the cycling championship.**
Je veux participer au championnat de cyclisme.
**I am an athlete so I must stay in shape.**
Je suis un athlète donc je dois rester en forme.
**After my boxing lesson, I want to go and swim in the pool.**
Après ma leçon de boxe, je veux aller nager dans la piscine.
**He will receive an award because he is the winner of the martial-arts tournament.**
Il recevra un prix car il est le vainqueur du tournoi d'arts martiaux.
**The wrestling captain must teach his team the rules of the sport.**
Le capitaine de catch doit enseigner à son équipe les règles du sport.
**At the horse-racing competition, the judge couldn't announce the score.**
Lors de la compétition de courses de chevaux, le juge n'a pas pu annoncer le score.
**There is a bicycle race at the park today.**
Il y a une course cycliste au parc aujourd'hui.
**This fitness program is expensive.**
Ce programme de remise en forme coûte cher.
**It's healthy to go to the gym every day.**
Il est sain d'aller au gymnase tous les jours.
**Weightlifting is good exercise.**
L'haltérophilie est un bon exercice.
**I want to run on the track today.**
Je veux courir sur la piste aujourd'hui.
**I like to win in billiards.**
J'aime gagner au billard.
**Skateboarding is forbidden here.**
Le skate est interdit ici.
**Skating is much easier than it seems.**
Le patinage est beaucoup plus facile qu'il n'y paraît.

# OUTDOOR ACTIVITIES - ACTIVITÉS EXTÉRIEURES

**Hiking** - Randonnée
**Hiking trail** - Sentier de randonnée
**Pocket knife** - Couteau de poche
**Compass** - Boussole
**Camping** - Camping / **A camp** - Un campement
**RV** - Camping-car
**Campground** - Camping
**Tent** - Tente
**Campfire** - Feu de camp / **Matches** - Allumettes / **Lighter** - Plus léger
**Coal** - Charbon
**Flame** - Flamme / **The smoke** - La fumée
**Fishing** - Pêche / **To fish** - Pêcher
**Fishing pole** - Canne à pêche / **Fishing line** - Fil de pêche
**Hook** - Hameçon, crochet / **A float** - Un flotteur / **A weight** - Un poids / **Bait** - Appât
**Fishing net** - Filet de pêche
**To hunt** - Chasser
**Rifle** - Fusil

**I enjoy hiking on the trail, with my compass and my pocketknife.**
J'aime faire de la randonnée sur le sentier, avec ma boussole et mon couteau de poche.
**Don't forget the water bottle in your backpack.**
N'oubliez pas la bouteille d'eau dans votre sac à dos.
**There aren't any tents at the campground.**
Il n'y a pas de tentes au camping.
**I want to sleep in an RV instead of a tent.**
Je veux dormir dans un camping-car au lieu d'une tente.
**We can use a lighter to start a campfire.**
Nous pouvons utiliser un briquet pour allumer un feu de camp.
**We need coal and matches for the camping trip.**
Nous avons besoin de charbon et d'allumettes pour le voyage de camping.
**Put out the fire because the flames are very high and there is a lot of smoke.**
Éteignez le feu car les flammes sont très hautes et il y a beaucoup de fumée.
**There is fog outside and the temperature is below freezing.**
Il y a du brouillard à l'extérieur et la température est en dessous de zéro.
**Where is the fishing store? I need to buy hooks, fishing line, bait, and a net.**
Où est le magasin de pêche? J'ai besoin d'acheter des hameçons, du fil de pêche, des appâts et un filet.
**You can't bring your fishing pole or your hunting rifle to the campground of the State Park because there is a sign there which says, "No fishing and no hunting."**
Vous ne pouvez pas apporter votre canne à pêche ou votre fusil de chasse au terrain de camping du parc d'État, car il y a un panneau indiquant «Pas de pêche et pas de chasse.»

**Sailing** - Voile
**A sail** - Un voilier
**Sailboat** - Voilier
**Rowing** - Aviron
**A paddle** - Une pagaie
**Motor** - Moteur
**Canoe** - Canoë
**Kayak** - Kayak
**Rock climbing** - Escalade
**Horseback riding** - Monter à cheval
**Diver** - Plongeur / **(f)** plongeuse
**Scuba diving** - Plongée sous-marine
**Skydiving** - Parachutisme
**Parachute** - Parachute
**Paragliding** - Parapente
**Hot air balloon** - Montgolfière
**Kite** - Kite
**Surfing** - Surfant / **Surf board** - Planche de surf
**Ice skating** - Patinage sur glace / **Skiing** - Ski

**With a broken motor, we need a paddle to row the boat.**
Avec un moteur cassé, nous avons besoin d'une pagaie pour ramer le bateau.
**It's important to know how to use a sail before sailing on a sailboat.**
Il est important de savoir utiliser une voile avant de naviguer sur un voilier.
**In my opinion, a kayak is much more fun than a canoe.**
À mon avis, un kayak est beaucoup plus amusant qu'un canot.
**Do I need to bring my scuba certification in order to scuba dive at the reef?**
Dois-je apporter ma certification de plongée pour faire de la plongée sous-marine sur le récif?
**I have my mask, snorkel, and fins.**
J'ai mon masque, mon tuba et mes palmes.
**I don't know which is scarier, sky diving or paragliding.**
Je ne sais pas ce qui est le plus effrayant, le parachutisme ou le parapente.
**There are several outdoor activities here including rock climbing and horseback riding.**
Il y a plusieurs activités de plein air ici, y compris l'escalade et l'équitation.
**My dream was always to fly in a hot-air balloon.**
Mon rêve était toujours de voler en montgolfière.
**We are going skiing on our next vacation.**
Nous allons skier lors de nos prochaines vacances.
**Where is the surfboard? I want to surf the waves at the beach tomorrow.**
Où est la planche de surf? Je veux surfer sur les vagues de la plage demain.
**Ice skating is fun.**
Le patinage sur glace est amusant.

# ELECTRICAL DEVICES - APPAREILS ÉLECTRIQUES

**Electricity** - Électricité / **Electric** - Électrique
**Appliance** - Appareil
**Oven** - Four
**Stove** - Le fourneau
**Microwave** - Micro onde
**Refrigerator** - Réfrigérateur / **Freezer** - Congélateur
**Coffee maker** - Machine à café / **Coffee pot** - Cafetière
**Toaster** - Grille-pain
**Dishwasher** - Lave-vaisselle
**Laundry machine** - Machine à laver / **Laundry** - Blanchisserie / **Dryer** - Séchoir
**Fan** - Ventilateur / **Air condition** - Air condition
**Alarm** - Alarme
**Smoke detector** - Détecteur de fumée
**Remote Control** - Télécommande
**Battery** - Batterie

**He needs to pay his electric bill if he wants electricity.**
Il doit payer sa facture d'électricité s'il veut de l'électricité.
**I need to purchase a few things at the electronic store and at the appliance store tomorrow.**
Je dois acheter quelques articles au magasin d'électronique et au magasin d'électroménagers demain.
**I can't put plastic utensils in the dishwasher.**
Je ne peux pas mettre d'ustensiles en plastique dans le lave-vaisselle.
**I am going to get rid of my microwave and oven because they are not functioning.**
Je vais me débarrasser de mon micro-ondes et de mon four car ils ne fonctionnent plus.
**The refrigerator and freezer aren't cold enough.**
Le réfrigérateur et le congélateur ne sont pas assez froids.
**The coffee maker and toaster aren't in the kitchen.**
La cafetière et le grille-pain ne sont pas dans la cuisine.
**My washing machine and dryer do not function therefore I must wash my laundry at the public laundromat.**
Ma machine à laver et mon sèche-linge ne fonctionnent pas, je dois donc laver mon linge à la laverie publique.
**Is this fan new?**
Ce ventilateur est-il nouveau?
**Unfortunately, the new air conditioner unit hasn't been delivered yet.**
Malheureusement, le nouveau climatiseur n'a pas encore été livré.
**Is that annoying sound the alarm clock or the fire alarm?**
Ce son ennuyeux est-il le réveil ou l'alarme d'incendie?
**The smoke detector needs new batteries.**
Le détecteur de fumée a besoin de nouvelles piles.

**Lamp -** Lampe
**Stereo -** Stéréo
**A clock -** Une horloge / **A watch -** Une montre
**Vacuum cleaner -** Aspirateur
**Phone -** Téléphone/**Text message -** Message texte/**Voice message -** Messagerie vocale
**Camera -** Caméra
**Flashlight -** Lampe de poche / **Light -** Lumière
**Furnace -** Fourneau / **Heater -** Chauffe-eau
**Cord -** Corde / **Charger -** Chargeur
**Outlet -** Sortie
**Headsets -** Écouteurs
**Door bell -** Cloche de porte
**Lawn mower -** Tondeuse à gazon

**The clock is hanging on the wall.**
L'horloge est accrochée au mur.
**The cordless stereo is on the table.**
La stéréo sans fil est sur la table.
**I still have a home telephone.**
J'ai toujours un téléphone à la maison.
**I need to buy a lamp and a vacuum cleaner today.**
J'ai besoin d'acheter une lampe et un aspirateur aujourd'hui.
**In the past, cameras were more common. Today, everyone can use their phones to take pictures.**
Dans le passé, les caméras étaient plus courantes. Aujourd'hui, tout le monde peut utiliser son téléphone pour prendre des photos.
**You can leave me a voice message or send me a text message.**
Vous pouvez me laisser un message vocal ou m'envoyer un message texte.
**The lights don't function when there is a blackout therefore I must rely on my flashlight.**
Les lumières ne fonctionnent pas en cas de panne de courant, je dois donc me fier à ma lampe de poche.
**I can't hear the doorbell.**
Je n'entends pas la sonnette.
**There is a higher risk of causing a house fire from an electric heater than a furnace.**
Il y a un risque plus élevé de provoquer un incendie de maison avec un radiateur électrique qu'une fournaise.
**I need to connect the cord to the outlet.**
J'ai besoin de connecter le cordon à la prise.
**His lawnmower is very noisy.**
Sa tondeuse à gazon est très bruyante.
**Why is my headset on the floor?**
Pourquoi mon casque est-il au sol?

# TOOLS - OUTILS

**Toolbox** - Boîte à outils
**Carpenter** - Charpentier
**Hammer** - Marteau
**Saw** - Scie / **Axe** - Hache
**A drill** - Une perceuse / **To drill** - Forer
**Nail** - Clou / **A screw** - Une vis
**Screwdriver** - Tournevis / **A wrench** - Une clé anglais / **Pliers** - Pinces
**Paint brush** - Pinceau / **To paint** - Peinturer / **The paint** - La peinture
**Ladder** - Échelle
**Rope** - Corde / **String** - Chaîne
**A scale** - Une échelle / **Measuring tape** - Mètre ruban
**Machine** - Machine
**A lock** - Un cadenas / **Locked** - Verrouillée / **To lock** - Verrouiller
**Equipment** - Équipement
**Broom** - Balai / **Dust pan** - Bac à poussière
**Mop** - Balai
**Bucket** - Seau / **Sponge** - Éponge
**Shovel** - Pelle / **A trowel** - Une truelle

**The carpenter needs nails, a hammer, a saw, and a drill.**
Le charpentier a besoin des clous, d'un marteau, d'une scie et d'une perceuse.
**The string is very long. Where are the scissors?**
La chaîne est très longue. Ou sont les ciseaux?
**The screwdriver is in the toolbox.**
Le tournevis est dans la boîte à outils.
**This tool can cut through metal.**
Cet outil peut couper le métal.
**The ladder is next to the tools.**
L'échelle est à côté des outils.
**I must buy a brush to paint the walls.**
Je dois acheter un pinceau pour peintre les murs.
**The paint bucket is empty.**
Le pot de peinture est vide.
**It's better to tie the shovel with a rope in my pick up truck.**
Il vaut mieux attacher la pelle avec une corde dans ma camionnette.
**How can I fix this machine?**
Comment puis-je réparer cette machine?
**The broom and dust pan are with the rest of my cleaning equipment.**
Le balai et le porte-poussière sont avec le reste de mon équipement de nettoyage.
**Where did you put the mop and the bucket?**
Où avez-vous mis la vadrouille et le seau?

# CAR - VOITURE

**Engine -** Moteur
**Ignition -** Allumage
**Steering wheel -** Volant
**Automatic -** Automatique
**Manual -** Manuelle
**Gear shift -** Changement de vitesse
**Seat -** Siège
**Seat belt -** Ceinture de sécurité
**Airbag -** Airbag
**Brakes -** Les freins
**Hand brake -** Frein à main
**Baby seat -** Siège bébé
**Driver seat -** Siège du conducteur
**Passenger seat -** Siège du passager
**Front seat -** Avant siège
**Back seat -** Arrière siège
**Car passenger -** Passager de voiture
**Warning light -** Lumière d'alarme
**Button -** Bouton / **Horn** (of the car) - Klaxon

**When driving, both hands must be on the steering wheel.**
Lorsque vous conduisez, les deux mains doivent être sur le volant.
**I must take my car to my mechanic because there is a problem with the ignition.**
Je dois amener ma voiture chez mon mécanicien car il y a un problème d'allumage.
**What happened to the engine?**
Qu'est-il arrivé au moteur?
**The seat is missing a seat belt.**
Il manque une ceinture de sécurité au siège.
**I prefer a gear shift instead of an automatic car.**
Je préfère un changement de vitesse plutôt qu'une voiture automatique.
**The brakes are new in this vehicle**
Les freins sont nouveaux dans ce véhicule
**This vehicle doesn't have a handbreak.**
Ce véhicule n'a pas de frein à main.
**There is an airbag on both the driver side and the passenger side.**
Il y a un airbag a côté du conducteur et a côté du passager.
**The baby seat is in the back seat.**
Le siège bébé est sur le siège d'arrière.
**The warning light button is located next to the stirring wheel.**
Le bouton du témoin lumineux est situé à côté du volant.

**Windshield** - Pare-brise
**Windshield wiper** - Essuie-glace
**Windshield fluid** - Liquide de pare-brise
**Rear view mirror** - Rétroviseur
**Side mirror** - Rétroviseur extérieur
**Door handle** - Poignée de porte
**Spare tire** - Pneu de rechange
**Trunk** - Coffre
**Hood** (of the vehicle) - Capot
**Alarm** - Alarme
**Window** - Fenêtre
**Drive license** - Permis de conduire
**License plate** - Plaque d'immatriculation
**Gas** - Gaz
**Low fuel** - Faible consommation de carburant
**Flat tire** - Pneu à plat
**Crowbar** - Crowbar
**A (car) jack** - Une prise
**Wrench** - Clé anglais

**The windshield and all four of my car windows are cracked.**
Le pare-brise et les quatre vitres de ma voiture sont cassé.
**I want to clean my rear-view mirror and my side mirrors.**
Je veux nettoyer mon rétroviseur et mes rétroviseurs extérieurs.
**My car doesn't have an alarm.**
Ma voiture n'a pas d'alarme.
**Does this car have a spare tire in the trunk?**
Cette voiture a-t-elle une roue de secours dans le coffre?
**Please, close the car door.**
Veuillez fermer la porte de la voiture.
**Where is the nearest gas station?**
Où est la station d'essence la plus proche?
**The windshield wipers are new.**
Les essuie-glaces sont neuves.
**The door handle on the driver's side is broken.**
La poignée de porte a côté du conducteur est cassée.
**Your license plate has expired.**
Votre plaque d'immatriculation a expiré.
**I want to renew my driving license today.**
Je veux renouveler mon permis de conduire aujourd'hui.
**Are the car doors locked?**
Les portes de la voiture sont-elles verrouillées?

# NATURE - LA NATURE

**A plant -** Une plante
**Forest -** Forêt
**Tree -** Arbre / **Wood -** Bois
**Trunk -** Tronc / **Branch -** Branche / **Leaf -** Feuille / **Root -** Racine
**Flower -** Fleur
**Petal -** Pétale
**Blossom -** Fleur
**Stem -** Tige / **Seed -** Grains
**Rose -** Rose
**Nectar -** Nectar / **Pollen -** Pollen
**Vegetation -** Végétation
**Bush -** Arbuste / **Grass -** Herbe
**Rain forest -** Forêt tropicale / **Tropical -** Tropical / **Palm tree -** Palmier
**Season -** Saison
**Spring -** Printemps /**Summer -** Été / **Winter -** Hiver / **Autumn -** L'automne

**I want to collect a few leaves during the fall.**
Je veux collecter quelques feuilles pendant l'automne.
**There aren't any plants in the desert during this season.**
Il n'y a pas de plantes dans le désert pendant cette saison.
**The trees need rain.**
Les arbres ont besoin de pluie.
**The trunk, the branches, and the roots are all parts of the tree.**
Le tronc, les branches et les racines sont toutes des parties de l'arbre.
**My rose bushes are beautiful.**
Mes rosiers sont magnifiques.
**Where can I plant the seeds?**
Où puis-je planter les grains?
**I must trim the grass in my garden.**
Je dois couper les herbes de mon jardin.
**The rain forest is a nature preserve.**
La forêt tropicale est une réserve naturelle.
**Palm trees can only grow in a tropical climate.**
Les palmiers ne peuvent pousser que dans un climat tropical.
**I am allergic to pollen.**
Je suis allergique au pollen.
**The orchid needs to bloom because I want to see its beautiful petals.**
L'orchidée a besoin de fleurir car je veux voir ses beaux pétales.
**Is the nectar from the flower sweet?**
Le nectar de la fleur est-il sucré?
**Be careful because the plant stem can break very easily.**
Soyez prudent car la tige de la plante peut se casser très facilement.

**Lake** - Lac
**Sea** - Mer
**Ocean** - Océan
**Waterfall** - Cascade
**River** - Rivière / **Canal** - Canal / **Swamp** - Marais
**Mountain** - Montagne / **Hill** - Colline / **Cliff** - Falaise / **Peak** - Sommet
**Rainbow** - Arc en ciel
**Cloud** - Nuage
**Lightning** - Un coup de foudre, éclair / **Thunder** - Tonnerre
**Rain** - Pluie / **Snow** - Neige
**Ice** - La glace / **Hail** - Grêle
**Fog** - Brouillard
**Wind** - Vent / **Air** - Air
**Dawn** - Aube / **Dew** - Rosée
**Sunset** - Coucher du soleil / **Sunrise** - Lever du soleil

**There is a rainbow above the waterfall.**
Il y a un arc-en-ciel au-dessus de la cascade.
**The ocean is bigger than the sea.**
L'océan est plus grand que la mer.
**From the mountain, I can see the river.**
De la montagne, je peux voir la rivière.
**Today we hope to see snow.**
Aujourd'hui, nous espérons voir de la neige.
**There aren't any clouds in the sky.**
Il n'y a pas de nuages dans le ciel.
**I see the lightning from my window.**
Je vois l'éclair de ma fenêtre.
**I can hear the thunder from outside.**
Je peux entendre le tonnerre de l'extérieur.
**I want to see the sunset from the hill.**
Je veux voir le coucher du soleil depuis la colline.
**The lake has a shallow part and a deep part.**
Le lac a une partie peu profonde et une partie tres profonde.
**I don't like the wind.**
Je n'aime pas le vent.
**The air on the mountain is very clear.**
L'air sur la montagne est très clair.
**Every dawn, there is dew on the leaves of my plants.**
Chaque aube, il y a de la rosée sur les feuilles de mes plantes.
**Is this ice or hail?**
Est-ce que ça cést de la glace ou de la grêle?
**I can see the volcano.**
Je peux voir le volcan.

## Nature

**Sky** - Ciel
**World** - Monde / **Earth** - Terre
**Sun** - Soleil / **Moon** - Lune / **Crescent** - Croissant / **Full moon** - Pleine lune
**Star** - Étoile / **Planet** - Planète
**Fire** - Feu / **Heat** - Chaleur / **Humidity** - Humidité
**Agriculture** - Agriculture
**Island** - Île
**Cave** - La grotte
**Public park** - Parc public / **National park** - Parc national
**Rock** - Roche / **Stone** - Pierre
**Ground / soil** - Sol
**Sea shore** - Bord de mer / **Seashell** - Coquillage
**Horizon** - Horizon
**Ray** - Rayon
**Dry** - Sec / **Wet** - Mouillè
**Deep** - Profond / **Shallow** - Peu profond
**Weeds** - Mauvaises herbes
**A stick** - Un baton
**Dust** - Poussière

**The moon and the stars are beautiful in the night sky.**
La lune et les étoiles sont magnifiques dans le ciel nocturne.
**The earth is a planet.**
La terre est une planète.
**The heat today is unbearable.**
Aujourd'hui, la chaleur est insupportable.
**At the beach there is fresh air.**
À la plage, il y a de l'air frais.
**I want to sail to the island to see the sunrise.**
Je veux naviguer vers l'île pour voir le lever du soleil.
**Parts of the cave are dry and other parts are wet.**
Certaines parties de la grotte sont sèches et d'autres parties sont mouillèes.
**We live in a beautiful world.**
Nous vivons dans un monde magnifique.
**There is dust from the fire in the park.**
Il y a de la poussière du feu dans le parc.
**I want to collect seashells from the seashore.**
Je veux ramasser des coquillages au bord de la mer.
**There are too many stones in the soil so it's impossible to use this area for agricultural purposes.**
Il y a trop de pierres dans le sol, il est donc impossible d'utiliser cette zone à des fins agricoles.
**Why are there so many weeds growing by the swamp?**
Pourquoi y a-t-il tant de mauvaises herbes qui poussent près de la marais?

# ANIMALS - ANIMAUX

**Animal -** Animal
**Pet -** Animal de compagnie
**Mammals -** Mammifères
**Dog -** Chien, **(f)** chienne **/ Cat -** Chat, **(f)** chatte
**Parrot -** Perroquet
**Pigeon -** Pigeon / colombe
**Pig -** Cochon
**Sheep -** Mouton **/ (m)** brebis
**Cow -** Vache **/ Bull -** Taureau
**Donkey -** Âne **/ Horse -** Cheval
**Camel -** Chameau
**Rodent -** Rongeur
**Mouse -** Souris **/ Rat -** Rat
**Rabbit -** Lapin, lièvre (hare) **/ Hamster -** Hamster
**Duck -** Canard **/ Goose -** Oie
**Turkey -** Dinde **/ Chicken -** Poulet, **(m)** Coq **/ Poultry -** La volaille
**Squirrel -** Écureuil

**I have a dog and two cats.**
J'ai un chien et deux chats.
**There is a bird on the tree.**
Il y a un oiseau sur l'arbre.
**I want to go to the zoo to see the animals.**
Je veux aller au zoo pour voir les animaux.
**My daughter wants a pet horse.**
Ma fille veut un cheval de compagnie.
**A pig, a sheep, a donkey, and a cow are considered farm animals.**
Un porc, un mouton, un âne et une vache sont considérés comme des animaux de ferme.
**I want a hamster as a pet.**
Je veux un hamster comme animal de compagnie.
**A camel is a desert animal.**
Un chameau est un animal du désert.
**Can I put ducks, geese, and turkeys inside my coop?**
Puis-je mettre des canards, des oies et des dindes dans ma cage?
**We have rabbits and squirrels in our yard.**
Nous avons des lapins et des écureuils dans notre cour.
**It's cruel to keep a parrot inside a cage.**
C'est cruel de garder un perroquet dans une cage.
**There are many pigeons in the city.**
Il y a beaucoup de pigeons dans la ville.
**Mice and rats are rodents.**
Les souris et les rats sont des rongeurs.

**Lion** - Lion, **(f)** lionne
**Hyena** - Hyène
**Leopard** - Léopard
**Panther** - Panthère
**Cheetah** - Guépard
**Elephant** - éléphant
**Rhinoceros** - Rhinocéros
**Hippopotamus** - Hippopotame
**Bat** - Chauve-souris
**Fox** - Renard / **Wolf** - Loup
**Weasel** - Belette
**Bear** - Ours
**Tiger** - Tigre
**Deer** - Cerf, **(f)** biche
**Monkey** - Singe / (f) guenon
**Otter** - Loutre
**Marsupial** - Marsupial

**There are a lot of animals in the forest.**
Il y a beaucoup d'animaux dans la forêt.
**The most dangerous animal in Africa is not the lion, it's the hippopotamus.**
L'animal le plus dangereux d'Afrique n'est pas le lion, c'est l'hippopotame.
**A wolf is much bigger than a fox.**
Un loup est beaucoup plus grand qu'un renard.
**Are there bears in this forest?**
Y a-t-il des ours dans cette forêt?
**Bats are the only mammals that can fly.**
Les chauves-souris sont les seuls mammifères qui peuvent voler.
**It's usually very difficult to see a leopard in the wild.**
Il est généralement très difficile de voir un léopard à l'état sauvage.
**Cheetahs are common in certain regions of Africa and rare in others.**
Les guépards sont communs dans certaines régions d'Afrique et rares dans d'autres.
**Elephants and rhinoceroses are known as very aggressive animals.**
Les éléphants et les rhinocéros sont connus comme des animaux très agressifs.
**I saw a hyena and a panther at the safari yesterday.**
Hier, j'ai vu une hyène et une panthère au safari.
**The largest member of the cat family is the tiger.**
Le plus grand membre de la famille des chats est le tigre.
**Deer hunting is forbidden in the national park.**
La chasse au cerf est interdite dans le parc national.
**There are many monkeys on the branches of the trees.**
Il y a beaucoup de singes sur les branches des arbres.
**An opossum isn't a rat but it's a marsupial just like the kangaroo.**
Un opossum n'est pas un rat mais c'est un marsupial tout comme le kangourou.

## Animals

**Bird** - Oiseau
**Crow** - Corbeau
**Stork** - Cigogne
**Vulture** - Vautour / **Eagle** - Aigle
**Owl** - Hibou
**Peacock** - Paon
**Reptile** - Reptile
**Turtle** - Tortue
**Snake** - Serpent
**Lizard** - Lézard / **Crocodile** - Crocodile
**Frog** - Grenouille
**Seal** - Joint
**Whale** - Baleine / **Dolphin** - Dauphin
**Fish** - Poisson
**Shark** - Requin
**Wing** - Aile / **Feather** - Plume
**Tail** - Queue
**Fur** - Fourrure
**Scales** - échelles / **Fins** - Palmes
**Horns** - Cornes
**Claws** - Les griffes

**An eagle and an owl are birds of prey however vultures are scavengers.**
Un aigle et un hibou sont des oiseaux de proie, mais les vautours sont des charognards.
**Crows are very smart.**
Les corbeaux sont très intelligents.
**I want to see the stork migration in Europe.**
Je veux voir la migration des cigognes en Europe.
**Don't buy a fur coat!**
N'achetez pas de manteau de fourrure!
**Butterflies and peacocks are colorful.**
Les papillons et les paons sont colorés.
**Some snakes are poisonous.**
Certains serpents sont poisoneux.
**Is that the sound of a cricket or a frog?**
Est-ce le son d'un grillon ou d'une grenouille?
**Lizards, crocodiles, and turtles belong to the reptile family.**
Les lézards, les crocodiles et les tortues appartiennent à la famille des reptiles.
**I want to see the fish in the lake.**
Je veux voir les poissons dans le lac.
**There were a lot of seals basking on the beach last week.**
La semaine dernière il y avait beaucoup des phoques se prélassant sur la plage.
**A whale is not a fish.**
Une baleine n'est pas un poisson.

**Insect -** Insecte
**A cricket -** Un cricket
**Ant -** Fourmi / **Termite -** Termite
**A fly -** Une mouche
**Butterfly -** Papillon
**Worm -** Ver de terre
**Mosquito -** Moustique / **Flea -** Puce / **Lice -** Les poux
**Beetle -** Scarabée
**A roach -** Cafard
**Bee -** Abeille
**Spider -** Araignée / **Scorpion -** Scorpion
**Snail -** Escargot
**Invertebrates -** Invertébrés
**Shrimps -** Crevettes / **Clams -** Moules / **Crab -** Crabe
**Octopus -** Poulpe
**Starfish -** Étoile de mer
**Jellyfish -** Méduse

**An octopus has eight tentacles.**
Une pieuvre a huit tentacules.
**A jellyfish is a common dish in Asian culture.**
Une méduse est un plat commun dans la culture asiatique.
**The museum has a large collection of invertebrate fossils.**
Le musée possède une grande collection de fossiles d'invertébrés.
**I want to buy mosquito spray.**
Je veux acheter un spray anti-moustique.
**I need antiseptic for my bug bites.**
J'ai besoin d'un antiseptique pour mes morsures d'insectes.
**I hope there aren't any worms, ants, or flies in the bag of sugar.**
J'espère qu'il n'y a pas de vers, de fourmis ou de mouches dans le sac du sucre.
**I have crabs and starfish in my aquarium.**
J'ai des crabes et des étoiles de mer dans mon aquarium.
**Certain types of spiders and scorpions can be dangerous.**
Certains types d'araignées et de scorpions peuvent être dangereux.
**I need to call the exterminator because there are fleas, roaches, and termites in my house.**
J'ai besoin d'appeler l'exterminateur parce qu'il y a des puces, des cafards et des termites dans ma maison.
**Bees are very important for the environment.**
Les abeilles sont très importantes pour l'environnement.
**Is there a snail inside the shell?**
Y a-t-il un escargot à l'intérieur de la coquille?
**Beetles are my favorite insects.**
Les coléoptères sont mes insectes préférés.

# RELIGION, CELEBRATIONS, & CUSTOMS
# RELIGION, FÊTE, ET TRADITIONS

**God** - Dieu / **Bible** - Bible
**Old Testament** - L'Ancien Testament / **New Testament** - Nouveau Testament
**Adam** - Adam / **Eve** - Eve / **Garden of Eden** - Jardin d'Eden / **Heaven** - Ciel
**Angels** - Anges / **Priest** - Prêtre / **Priest** (in Judaism) - Cohen
**Noah** - Noé / **Ark** - Arche
**To pray** - Prier / **Prayer** - Prière
**Blessing** - Bénédiction / **To bless** - Bénir / **Holy** - Saint, (f) sainte / **Faith** - Foi
**Moses** - Moïse / **Prophet** - Prophète / **Messiah** - Messie / **Miracle** - Miracle
**Ten commandments** - Dix Commandements
**The five books of Moses** - Les cinq livres de Moïse
**Genesis** - Genèse / **Exodus** - Exode / **Leviticus** - Lévitique
**Numbers** - Nombres / **Deuteronomy** - Deutéronome

**What is your religion?**
Quelle est votre religion?
**The monotheistic faiths use the bible.**
Les religions monothéistes utilisent la Bible.
**We have faith in miracles.**
Nous avons foi aux miracles.
**When do I need to say the blessing?**
Quand dois-je dire la bénédiction?
**I must say a prayer for the holiday.**
Je dois dire une prière pour la fête.
**The angels came from heaven.**
Les anges sont venus du ciel.
**Aaron, the brother of Moses, was the first priest.**
Aaron, le frère de Moïse, était le premier prêtre.
**The story of Noah's Ark and the flood is very interesting.**
L'histoire de l'arche de Noé et du déluge est très intéressante.
**Adam and Eve were the first humans and they lived in the Garden of Eden.**
Adam et Eve ont été les premiers humains et ils ont vécu dans le jardin d'Eden.
**Moses had to climb up on Mount Sinai to receive the Ten Commandments from God.**
Moïse a dû monter sur le mont Sinaï pour recevoir les dix commandements de Dieu.
**The Five Books of the Moses are Genesis, Exodus, Leviticus, Numbers, and Deuteronomy.**
Les cinq livres de Moïse sont la Genèse, l'Exode, le Lévitique, les Nombres et le Deutéronome.
**Moses was considered as the prophet of all prophets.**
Moïse était considéré comme le prophète de tous les prophètes

**Christian Religion** - Religion chrétienne
**Church** - Église / **Cathedral** - Cathédrale
**Catholic** - catholique / **Christian** - Chrétien, **(f)** chrétienne
**Christianity** - Christianisme / **Catholicism** - Catholicisme
**Jesus** - Jésus / **A cross** - Croix
**Priest** - Prêtre / **Holy** - Saint / **Holy water** - Eau bénite
**To sin** - Pécher / **A sin** - Un péché
**Monastery** - Monastère
**Christmas** - Noël / **Christmas eve** - Réveillon de Noël
**Christmas tree** - Sapin de Noël
**New Year** - Nouvel An
**Merry Christmas** - Joyeux Noël
**Easter** - Pâques
**Saint** - Saint, **(f)** Sainte / **Nun** - Religieuse
**Chapel** - Chapelle

**The church is open today.**
L'église est ouverte aujourd'hui.
**Christians love to celebrate Christmas.**
Les chrétiens prient fêter Noël.
**I need to turn on the lights on my Christmas tree for Christmas Eve.**
Je dois allumer les lumières de mon sapin de Noël pour la veille de Noël.
**Two more weeks until Easter.**
Encore deux semaines jusqu'à Pâques.
**The nuns live in the monastery.**
Les religieuses vivent dans le monastère.
**The priest read a psalm from the Bible in front of the congregation.**
Le prêtre a lu un psaume de la Bible devant l'assemblée.
**I went to pray in the cathedral.**
Je suis allé prier dans la cathédrale.
**Jesus is the son of God.**
Jésus est le fils de Dieu.
**I have a gold necklace with a cross.**
J'ai un collier en or avec une croix.
**Merry Christmas and Happy New Year to all my friends and family.**
Joyeux Noël et bonne année à tous mes amis et à ma famille.
**Peter is a famous saint in Christianity.**
Pierre est un saint célèbre dans le christianisme.
**The priest baptized the baby in the holy water.**
Le prêtre a baptisé le bébé dans l'eau bénite.
**The devil and the demons are from hell.**
Le diable et les démons viennent de l'enfer.
**Many schools refuse to teach evolution.**
Des nombreuses écoles refusent d'enseigner l'évolution.

**Jew -** Juif, **(f)** juive / **Judaism -** Judaïsme
**Religious -** Religieux / **(f)** religieuse
**Monotheism -** Monothéisme
**Synagogue -** Synagogue
**Kosher -** Kascher
**Passover -** Pâque
**Menorah -** Menorah
**Dreidle -** Toupis
**Goblet -** Gobelet
**Wine -** Du vin
**Circumcision -** Circoncision
**Islam -** Islam / **Muslim -** Musulman, **(f)** musulmane
**Mosque -** Mosquée
**Hindu -** Hindou / **Buddhist -** Bouddhiste
**Temple -** Temple

**The Jews worship at the synagogue.**
Les Juifs prient dans la synagogue.
**The Bible is a holy book which tells the story of the Jewish nations and includes many miracles.**
La Bible est un livre sacré qui raconte l'histoire des nations juives et comprend de nombreux miracles.
**In Judaism, they pray three times a day. Morning prayer, afternoon prayer, and evening prayer.**
Dans le judaïsme, ils prient trois fois par jour. Prière du matin, prière de l'après-midi et prière du soir.
**The three forefathers are Abraham, Isaac, and Jacob.**
Les trois ancêtres sont Abraham, Isaac et Jacob.
**Where is the goblet of wine for Rosh Hashana?**
Où est le gobelet de vin pour Roch Hachana?
**I have a menorah and a dreidel for Hannukah.**
J'ai une menorah et un toupis pour Hanoukka.
**Passover is my favorite holiday.**
La Pâque est ma fête préférée.
**We welcome the Sabbath by lighting candles.**
Nous accueillons le shabbat en allumant des bougies.
**I want to keep kosher.**
Je veux observer le casher.
**To learn about the Holocaust and the concentration camps is very important.**
Il est très important de se renseigner sur l'Holocauste et les camps de concentration.
**Muslims pray at the mosque.**
Les musulmans prient à la mosquée.
**In Islam they must pray five times a day.**
Dans l'Islam, ils doivent prier cinq fois par jour.

Politics

# WEDDING AND RELATIONSHIP
# MARIAGE ET RELATION

**Wedding** - Mariage
**Wedding hall** - Salle de mariage
**Married** - Mariés
**Civil wedding** - Mariage civil
**Bride** - La mariée
**Groom** - Le marié
**Ceremony** - La cérémonie
**Reception** - Réception
**Chapel** - Chapelle
**Engagement** - Engagement
**Engagement ring** - Bague de fiançailles
**Wedding ring** - La bague de mariage
**Anniversary** - Anniversaire
**Honeymoon** - Voyage de noces
**Fiancé** - Fiancé / **(f)** fiancée
**Husband** - Mari
**Wife** - Femme

**When is the wedding?**
Quand est le mariage?
**We are having the service in the chapel and the reception in the wedding hall.**
Nous avons le service dans la chapelle et la réception dans la salle de mariage.
**Our anniversary is on Valentine's Day.**
Notre anniversaire est le jour de la Saint-Valentin.
**This is my engagement ring and this is my wedding ring.**
Ceci est ma bague de fiançailles et ceci est ma bague de mariage.
**They are finally married so now it's time for the honeymoon.**
Ils sont finalement mariés alors maintenant il est temps pour la lune de miel.
**He decided to propose to his girlfriend. She said "yes" and now they are engaged.**
Il a décidé de proposer à sa petite amie. Elle a dit "oui" et maintenant ils sont fiancés.
**He is my fiancé now. Next year he will be my husband.**
Il est mon fiancé maintenant. L'année prochaine, il sera mon mari.
**Three civil weddings are taking place at the courthouse today.**
Trois mariages civils ont lieu au palais de justice aujourd'hui.
**The bride and groom received many presents.**
La mariée et le marié ont reçu de nombreux cadeaux.

**Valentine day** - Saint Valentin
**Love** - L'amour **/ To love** - Aimer
**In love** - Amoureux
**Romantic** - Romantique
**Darling** - Chéri / **(f)** chérie
**A date** - Un rendez-vous
**A** (romantic) **relationship** - Une relation
**A** (non-romantic) **relationship** - Une relation
**Boyfriend** - Petit ami
**Girlfriend** - Petite amie
**To hug** - Embrasser
**A hug** - Un câlin
**To kiss** - Embrasser
**A kiss** - Un bisou
**Single** - Célibataire
**Divorced** - Divorcé / **(f)** divorcée
**Widow** - Veuf / **(f)** veuve

**I am in love with her.**
Je suis amoureux d'elle.
**I am in love with him.**
Je suis amoureuse de lui.
**I love her** (male to female).
Je l'aime.
**I love him** (female to male).
Je l'aime.
**I love you.**
Je t'aime.
**You are very romantic.**
Tu es très romantique.
**They have a very good relationship.**
Ils ont une très bonne relation.
**The husband and wife are in a relationship.**
Le mari et la femme sont un couple.
**I am single because I divorced my wife.**
Je suis célibataire parce que j'ai divorcé ma femme.
**She is my darling and my love.**
Elle est ma chérie et mon amour.
**I want to kiss you and hug you in this picture.**
Je veux te donner un bisou et t'embrasser sur cette photo.

# POLITICS - POLITIQUE

**Politics** - Politique
**Flag** - Drapeau
**National anthem** - Hymne national
**Nation** - Nation
**National** - National
**International** - International
**Local** - Local
**Patriot** - Patriot
**Symbol** - Symbole
**Peace** - Paix
**Treaty** - Traité
**State** - État
**Country** - Pays
**County** - Comté
**Century** - Siècle
**Majority** - Majorité
**Local** - Local
**Campaign** - Campagne
**Annexation** - Annexion
**Startegic** - Stratégique
**Plan** - Plan
**Decision** - Décision

**This is a political movement which is supported by the majority.**
Il s'agit d'un mouvement politique soutenu par la majorité.
**This flag is the national symbol of the country.**
Ce drapeau est le symbole national du pays.
**This is all politics.**
C'est toute la politique.
**There is a difference between state law and local law.**
Il y a une différence entre la loi de l'État et la loi locale.
**He is a patriot of the nation.**
C'est un patriote de la nation.
**Most countries have a national anthem.**
La plupart des pays ont un hymne national.
**This is a political campaign to demand independence.**
Il s'agit d'une campagne politique pour exiger l'indépendance.
**The annexation plan was a strategic decision.**
Le plan d'annexion était une décision stratégique.

**Legal -** Légal
**Law -** Loi
**Illegal -** Illégal
**International law -** La loi internationale
**Human rights -** Droits humains
**Punishment -** Châtiment / punition
**Torture -** Torture
**Execution** (to kill) **-** Exécution
**Spy -** Espion
**Amnesty -** Amnistie
**Political asylum -** L'asile politique
**Republic -** République
**Dictator -** Dictateur
**Citizen -** Citoyen / **(f)** citoyenne
**Resident -** Résident / **(f)** résidente
**Immigrant -** Immigrant / **(f)** immigrante
**Public -** Public / **Private -** Privé
**Racism -** Racisme
**Government -** Gouvernement
**Revolution -** Révolution
**Civilian -** Civil
**Population -** Population
**Socialism -** Socialisme
**Communism -** Communisme

**There were many protests and riots today.**
Il y a eu de nombreuses manifestations et émeutes aujourd'hui.
**The civilian population wanted a revolution.**
La population civile voulait une révolution.
**The politicians want to ask the president to give the captured spy amnesty.**
Les politiciens veulent demander au président d'accorder l'amnistie de l'espion capturé.
**Although he was the brutal dictator of the republic, in private he was a nice person.**
Bien qu'il ait été le dictateur brutal de la république, en privé, il était une bonne personne.
**In some countries torture and execution is a common form of legitimate punishment.**
Dans certains pays, la torture et l'exécution sont une forme courante de punition légitime.
**This is a violation of human rights and international law.**
Il s'agit d'une violation des droits de l'homme et du droit international.
**Communism and socialism were popular in the 19th century.**
Le communisme et le socialisme étaient populaires au 19e siècle.
**In which county is this legal?**
Dans quel comté est-ce légal?

**President -** Président
**Statement -** Déclaration
**Presidential -** Présidentiel
**Vice president -** Vice président
**Defense minister -** Ministre de la défense
**Interior minister -** Ministre de l'Intérieur
**Exterior minister -** Ministre de l'extérieur
**Prime minister -** Premier ministre
**Election -** Élection
**Poll -** Sondage
**Campaign -** Campagne
**Candidate -** Candidat
**Democracy -** La démocratie
**Movement -** Mouvement
**Politician -** Politicien / **(f)** politicienne
**Politics -** Politique
**To vote -** Voter
**Majority -** Majorité
**Independence -** Indépendance
**Party -** Formation / partie
**Veto -** Veto
**Impeachment -** Mise en accusation
**Convoy -** Convoi

**They want to appoint him as defense minister.**
Ils veulent le nommer ministre de la défense.
**Both parties want to veto the impeachment inquiry.**
Les deux parties veulent opposer leur veto à l'enquête sur la destitution.
**I want to see the presidential convoy.**
Je veux voir le convoi présidentiel.
**In some countries other than the United States, they have a prime minister, interior minister, and exterior minister.**
Dans certains pays autres que les États-Unis, ils ont un premier ministre, un ministre de l'intérieur et un ministre de l'extérieur.
**I want to meet the president and the vice president.**
Je veux rencontrer le président et le vice-président.
**I want to go to the election polls to vote for the new candidate.**
Je veux aller aux urnes des élections pour voter le nouveau candidat.
**We support democracy and are against fascism and racism.**
Nous soutenons la démocratie et sommes contre le fascisme et le racisme.

**United Nations** - Les Nations Unies
**Condemnation** - Condamnation
**United States** - États Unis
**European Union** - Union européenne
**Coup** - Coup d'etat
**Treason** - Trahison
**Fascism** - Fascisme
**Resistance** - La résistance
**Members** - Membres
**Captured** - Capturé / **To capture** - Capturer
**Ambassador** - Ambassadeur / **(f)** ambassadrice
**Embassy** - Ambassade
**Consulate** - Consulat
**Biased** - Biais
**Unilateral** - Unilatéral
**Bilateral** - Bilatéral
**Resolution** - Résolution
**Rebels** - Rebelles
**Sanctions** - Les sanctions

**All the members of the resistance were accused of treason and had to ask for political asylum.**
Tous les membres de la résistance ont été accusés de trahison et ont dû demander l'asile politique.
**The resolution is biased.**
La résolution est biaisée.
**This was an official condemnation.**
C'était une condamnation officielle.
**The United Nations is located in New York.**
Les Nations Unies sont situées à New York.
**I am a United States citizen and a resident of the European Union.**
Je suis citoyen américain et résident de l'Union européenne.
**This is the ambassador's residence is located near the embassy.**
C'est la résidence de l'ambassadeur qui est située près de l'ambassade.
**I need the phone number and address of the consulate.**
J'ai besoin du numéro de téléphone et de l'adresse du consulat.
**Are consular services available today?**
Des services consulaires sont-ils disponibles aujourd'hui?
**The international peace treaty needs to include both sides.**
Le traité de paix international doit inclure les deux parties.
**According to the government, the rebels carried out an illegal coup.**
Selon le gouvernement, les rebelles ont perpétré un coup d'État illégal.
**They must impose sanctions against that country.**
Ils doivent imposer des sanctions contre ce pays.

# MILITARY - MILITAIRE

**Army** - Armée / **Armed forces** - Forces armées
**Navy** - Marin
**Soldier** Soldat / **Troops** - Troupes
**A force** - Une force / **Ground forces** - Forces terrestres
**Base** - Base / **Headquarter** - Siège social / **Intelligence** - Intelligence
**Ranks** - Rangs / **Sergeant** - Sergent / **Lieutenant** - Lieutenant
**The general** - Le général / **Commander** - Le commandant / **Colonel** - Colonel
**Military chief of Staff** - Chef d'état-major militaire
**Enlistment** - Enrôlement
**Reserves** - Réserves
**War** - Guerre
**Terrorism** - Terrorisme / **Terrorist** - Terroriste / **Insurgency** - Insurrection
**Border crossing** - Poste frontière
**Refugee** - Réfugié / **(f)** réfugiée
**Camp** - Camp

**I want to enlist in the military.**
Je veux m'enrôler dans l'armée.
**This base is designated for military aircrafts only.**
Cette base est réservée aux avions militaires uniquement.
**That is the headquarters of the enemy.**
C'est le quartier général de l'ennemi.
**This country has a powerful airforce.**
Ce pays a une puissante force aérienne.
**They need to enlist reserve forces for the war.**
Ils doivent enrôler des forces de réserve pour la guerre.
**Welcome to the border crossing.**
Bienvenue au poste frontalier.
**Military intelligence relies on important sources of information.**
Le renseignement militaire s'appuie sur d'importantes sources d'information.
**The military chief of staff was the target of a failed assassination attempt.**
Le chef d'état-major militaire a été la cible d'une tentative d'assassinat ratée.
**The sniper killed the highest-ranking lieutenant.**
Le tireur d'élite a tué le plus haut gradé lieutenant.
**The terrorist group claimed responsibility for the car-bomb attack at the refugee camp.**
Le groupe terroriste a revendiqué la responsabilité de l'attentat à la voiture piégée dans le camp de réfugiés.
**It's impossible to defeat terrorism because it's an ideology.**
Il est impossible de vaincre le terrorisme car c'est une idéologie.

**Air strike** - Frappe aérienne
**Air force** - Armée de l'air / **Fighter jet** - Avion de chasse
**Military aircraft** - Avions militaires
**Drone** - Drone / **Stealth technology** - Technologie furtive
**Tank** - Char
**Submarine** - Sous-marin
**Weapon** - Arme
**Grenade** - Grenade / **Mine** - Mine / **Bomb** - Bombe / **Explosion** - Explosion
**Sniper** - Tireur d'élite / **Gun** - Pistolet / **Rifle** - Fusil / **Bullet** - Balle
**Missile** - Missile / **Mortar** - Mortier
**Anti tank missile** - Missile antichar / **Anti aircraft missile** - Missile antiaérien
**Shoulder fire missile** - Missile de tir d'épaule
**Ammunition** - Munition / **Artillery** - Artillerie / **Artillery shell** - Obus d'artillerie
**Precision missile** - Missile de précision / **Ballistic missile** - Missile balistique
**Atomic bomb** - Bombe atomique / **Nuclear weapon** - Arme nucléaire
**Weapon of mass destruction** - Arme de destruction massive
**Chemical weapon** - Arme chimique
**Flare system** - Système Flare
**Supply** - La fourniture / **Storage** - Espace de rangement
**Armor** - Armure

**The M-16 is a US-made rifle.**
Le M-16 est un fusil de fabrication américaine.
**The tank fired artillery shells.**
Le char a tiré des obus d'artillerie.
**Shoulder-fired missiles are extremely dangerous and are hard to defend against.**
Les missiles à l'épaule sont extrêmement dangereux et difficiles à défendre.
**The flare system is meant as a defense against anti-aircraft missiles.**
Le système de fusée éclairante est conçu comme une défense contre les missiles antiaériens.
**The navy was able to intercept a missile.**
La marine a pu intercepter un missile.
**At the terrorist safe-house, guns, bullets, and grenades were found.**
Au refuge des terroristes ont été trouvés, des fusils, des balles et des grenades.
**The coalition forces struck an enemy arms depot.**
Les forces de la coalition ont frappé un dépôt d'armes ennemi.
**An intense missile attack was carried out against the supply forces that resulted in many casualties.**
Une intense attaque de missiles a été menée contre les forces d'approvisionnement, faisant de nombreuses victimes.
**The terrorist cell fired ballistic missiles at the nuclear facility site.**
La cellule terroriste a tiré des missiles balistiques sur le site d'installation nucléaire.
**Atomic bombs and chemical weapons are weapons of mass destruction.**
Les bombes atomiques et les armes chimiques sont des armes de destruction massive.

# Military

**A target** - Une cible / **To target** - Cibler
**An attack** - Une attaque / **To attack** - Attaquer
**Intense** - Intense
**To shoot** - Tirer / **To open fire** - Ouvrir le feu / **Fired** - Tiré
**Assassination** - Assassinat / **Assassin** - Assassin
**Enemy** - Ennemi
**Reconnaissance** - Reconnaissance / **To infiltrate** - Infiltrer / **Invasion** - Invasion
**Exchange of fire** - Échange de feu
**A cease fire** - Un cessez-le-feu / **Withdrawal** - Retrait
**To defeat** - Vaincu
**To surrender** - Se rendre
**Victim** - Victime
**Injury** - Blessure / **Deaths** - Des morts / **To kill** - Tuer
**Prisoner of war** - Prisonnier de guerre
**Missing in action** - Disparu au combat
**Act of war** - Acte de guerre
**War crimes** - Crimes de guerre
**Defense** - La défense
**Attempt** - Tentative

There is an invasion of ground forces.
Il y a une invasion des forces terrestres.
The soldier wanted to open fire and shoot at the invading forces.
Le soldat a voulu ouvrir le feu et tirer sur les forces d'invasion.
The bomb attack was considered an act of aggression and an act of war.
L'attentat à la bombe a été considéré comme un acte d'agression et un acte de guerre.
The reconnaissance drone managed to infiltrate deep within enemy territory.
Le drone de reconnaissance a réussi à s'infiltrer profondément en territoire de l'ennemi.
The airstrike targeted an ammunition storage site.
La frappe aérienne a visé un site de stockage de munitions.
The mortar attack and exchange of fire caused injuries and deaths on both sides.
L'attaque au mortier et l'échange de tirs ont fait des blessés et des morts des deux côtés.
First, we need to clear the mines.
Premièrement, nous devons nettoyer les mines.
The ceasefire agreement included the release of prisoners of war.
L'accord de cessez-le-feu prévoyait la libération des prisonniers de guerre.
The army made a public statement to announce the withdrawal.
L'armée a fait une déclaration publique pour annoncer le retrait.
There was a huge explosion as a result of the terrorist attack.
Il y a eu une énorme explosion à la suite de l'attaque terroriste.
The commander of the insurgency was accused of serious war crimes.
Le commandant de l'insurrection a été accusé de graves crimes de guerre.
Several of the submarine sailors were missing in action.
Plusieurs sous-marins étaient portés disparus au combat.

# Basic Grammatical Requirements of the French Language

## *Adjectives

In English, adjectives precede the noun, but in French, it's usually the opposite. Fast car will be *voiture rapide,* cold winter will be *hiver froid.*

French adjectives are modified by the number and gender of the nouns which they are pertaining to. Every adjective can have four forms.

- \* To use with a masculine noun, you leave it the way it is.
- \* To use with a feminine noun, just add an e at the end.
- \* To make it plural masculine, add an *s* at the end.
- \* To make it plural feminine, then simply add *es* at the end.

For example: smart, intelligent; he is smart will be *il est intelligent,* she is smart *elle est intelligente,* plural masculine, *ils sont intelligents* / plural feminine, *ils sont intelligentes.*

But if the adjective ends with an *s* or *x*, then for masculine plural, add nothing, but for feminine, you must replace the *x* at the end with *se*, and for feminine plural, you replace it with *ses*.

- \* "he is happy" / *il est heureux*
- \* "she is happy" / *elle est heureuse*
- \* "the boys are happy" / *les garçons sont heureux*
- \* "the girls are happy" / *les filles sont heureuses*

## Comparisons

In order to use comparisons, add *plus* and *que*. For example:

- \* "darker than" / *plus sombre que*
- \* "stronger than" / *plus forte que*

## Time

When referring to time, *il est une heure* means "it's one o'clock." Any number greater than one, the *heure* becomes pluralized:

- \* *il est cinq heures* / "it's five o'clock"
- \* *il est six heures* / "it's six o'clock"

Basic Grammatical Requirements of French

## Verbs

French verbs are conjugated in a different form than English verbs. To make a verb negative, add *ne* before the verb and *pas* after. For example:

- \* I don't want / *je ne veux pas*

- \* I don't see / *je ne vois pas*
- \* I can't / *je ne peux pas*
- \* I don't like / *je n'aime pas*

Since *aime* ("like") begins with a vowel, the *e* in *ne* is eliminated, and it connects to the verb with an apostrophe.

\*a contraction is used when the word which follows *ne* begins with a vowel)

## Demonstratives

"This" (*ceci*) and "that" (*cela*) are the formal ways of reference to "this" and "that." But instead, use *ce* and *ça*, which are the spoken form. Both *ce* (*cette*, feminine tense of *ce*, and *ces* is the plural of *ce* and *cette*) and *ça* could mean the same thing: "this," "that," and "it." The difference between the two is that *ce* usually goes with a noun, neutral, or the verb *être* ("to be").

Noun:
- \* "that place" / *ce lieu*
- \* "that house" / *cette maison*
- \* "these days" / *ces jours*

Verb *être* ("to be"):
- \* "that is a boy" / *c'est un garçon*
- \* "that is very easy" / *c'est très facile*
- \* "it is not impossible" / *ce n'est pas impossible*

Since "is" is a form of the verb "to be," "that is" or "this is" (both words connect) *ce* +*est* =*c'est*, 'it's not" or "this/that is not" is *ce n'est*.

Neutral:
- \* "this idea" / *cette idée*
- \* "that journey" / *ce voyage*

"Idea" and "journey" are neutral since they can be either male or female.

*Ça* usually goes with any other verb besides *être*:
- \* "I want this" / *je veux ça*
- \* "I don't need this" / *je n'ai pas besoin de ça*

\* Both *ce* and *ça* can also be used before the verbs *pouvoir* and *devoir*:
- \* "this can be hard" / *ce peut être difficile*
- \* "this must happen" / *ce doit faire*
- \* "this can be hard" / *ça peut être difficile*
- \* "this must happen" / *ça doit faire*

Basic Grammatical Requirements of the French Language

## Reading and Pronunciation in the French Language

French pronunciation is rather different than English, because there are multiple ways in which letters can become silent. But if you follow these following steps, it will help you in French pronunciation.

In general, most consonants in English and French sound the same.

*Ge* and *gi* is pronounced as "je."

*H* is silent.

*Qu* is pronounced as "k."

*Ch* is pronounced as "shhhhh."

*Th* is pronounced as "t," rather than being pronounced as "th."

Ç and the *r* in the French language are letters that don't exist in English. The *ç* sounds like an *s*. The French *r*, on the other hand, is pronounced at the back of your throat, unlike the *r* in English and Spanish.

## Pronouncing Vowels in French

*E* sounds like "e" in "bed."
*É* sounds like "ay" as in "day."
*Ê, È* sounds like "e" in "net."
*I, Y* sounds like "ee."

## Diphthongs

*Ail* sounds like "i" in "night."
*An, en,* and *em* are pronounced with a long nasal sound.
*Oi* sounds like "wa."
*Oui* sounds like "wee."
*O, au,* and *eau* sound like the "o" in float."
*Ou* sounds like "oo" in "pool."
*U* is pronounced by rounding the mouth like an "o" and saying the letter "e."

## Silent Letters

The French language has silent letters that can be divided into three categories:
* E muet / elision
* H muet and aspiré
* Final consonants

In French, with words that end with an "e," the "e" is usually not pronounced, but the consonant that precedes it is. For example, *belle* is pronounced as "bell," *porte* is pronounced as "port." The letter "h" is never pronounced and is silent.

**The Elision Rule** applies to words ending in *ce, je, me, te, se, de, ne, que*, in which the last letter is omitted, as long as the following word begins with a consonant, and both connect creating one syllable:

* "I love you" / je t'aime
* "I have" / j'ai
* "I don't have" / je n'ai pas

In French, the final consonant is dropped unless there is a "c," "f," or "l," all of which are generally pronounced. For example, *bijoux* is pronounced as *bijou*, *tous* is pronounced as *tou*, *veux* is pronounced as *veu*. In the event a noun or adjective is pluralized, the "s" will be dropped as well. For example, "cat" *chat* is pronounced as *cha*, but the plural *chats* is pronounced as *chat*. Another example: "*Dans,*" meaning "in," is pronounced as *dan* (the "n" should not be stressed too strongly). There are a few exceptions though, including *avec, club, hiver, avril,* and a few others as well.

The Liaison Rule is a situation in which a consonant at the end of a word that would usually not be pronounced is pronounced because it's followed by a word that begins with a vowel or silent "h." In that situation, the "s" or "x" are pronounced as "z." "The friends," *les amis*, is pronounced as *lez-amis*. *Deux amis* is pronounced as *deuz-amis*.

# Conclusion

Hopefully, you have enjoyed this book and will use the knowledge you have learned in various situations in your everyday life. In contrast to other methods of learning foreign languages, the theory in this current usage is that ever-greater topics can be broached so that one's vocabulary can expand. This method relies on the discovery I made of the list of core words from each language. Once these are learned, your conversational learning skills will progress very quickly.

You are now ready to discuss sport and school and office-related topics and this will open up your world to a more satisfying extent. Humans are social creatures and language helps us interact. Indeed, at times, it can keep us alive, such as in war situations. You might find yourself in dangerous situations perhaps as a journalist, military personnel or civilian and you need to be armed with the appropriate vocabulary.

"This is a base for military aircraft only," you may have to tell some people who try to enter a field you are protecting, or know what you are being told when someone says to you, "Welcome to the border crossing." As a journalist on a foreign assignment, you may need to quickly understand what you are being told, such as "The sniper killed the highest-ranking lieutenant." If you are someone negotiating on behalf of the army, you may need to find another lieutenant very quickly. Lives, at times, literally depend on your level of understanding and comprehension.

This unique approach that I first discovered when using this method to learn on my own, will have helped you speak the French language much quicker than any other way.

# NOTE FROM THE AUTHOR

Thank you for your interest in my work. I encourage you to share your overall experience of this book by posting a review. Your review can make a difference! Please feel free to describe how you benefited from my method or provide creative feedback on how I can improve this program. I am constantly seeking ways to enhance the quality of this product, based on personal testimonials and suggestions from individuals like you. In order to post a review, please check with the retailer of this book.

Thanks and best of luck,<br>
Yatir Nitzany

www.ingramcontent.com/pod-product-compliance
Lightning Source LLC
Chambersburg PA
CBHW050334120526
44592CB00014B/2174